MznLnx

Missing Links Exam Preps

Exam Prep for

Elementary Algebra

Bittinger & Ellenbogen, 6th Edition

The MznLnx Exam Prep is your link from the texbook and lecture to your exams.
The MznLnx Exam Preps are unauthorized and comprehensive reviews of your textbooks.

All material provided by MznLnx and Rico Publications (c) 2010
Textbook publishers and textbook authors do not particpate in or contribute to these reviews.

MznLnx

Rico
Publications

Exam Prep for Elementary Algebra
6th Edition
Bittinger & Ellenbogen

Publisher: Raymond Houge
Assistant Editor: Michael Rouger
Text and Cover Designer: Lisa Buckner
Marketing Manager: Sara Swagger
Project Manager, Editorial Production: Jerry Emerson
Art Director: Vernon Lowerui

Product Manager: Dave Mason
Editorial Asitant: Rachel Guzmanji
Pedagogy: Debra Long
Cover Image: Jim Reed/Getty Images
Text and Cover Printer: City Printing, Inc.
Compositor: Media Mix, Inc.

(c) 2010 Rico Publications
ALL RIGHTS RESERVED. No part of this work
covered by the copyright may be reproduced or
used in any form or by an means--graphic, electronic,
or mechanical, including photocopying, recording,
taping, Web distribution, information storage, and
retrieval systems, or in any other manner--without the
written permission of the publisher.

Printed in the United States
ISBN:

For more information about our products, contact us at:
Dave.Mason@RicoPublications.com

For permission to use material from this text or
product, submit a request online to:
Dave.Mason@RicoPublications.com

Contents

CHAPTER 1
Introduction to Algebraic Expressions — 1

CHAPTER 2
Equations, Inequalities, and Problem Solving — 9

CHAPTER 3
Introduction to Graphing — 13

CHAPTER 4
Polynomials — 15

CHAPTER 5
Polynomials and Factoring — 23

CHAPTER 6
Rational Expressions and Equations — 27

CHAPTER 7
Systems and More Graphing — 32

CHAPTER 8
Radical Expressions and Equations — 34

CHAPTER 9
Quadratic Equations — 40

ANSWER KEY — 47

TO THE STUDENT

COMPREHENSIVE

The *MznLnx* Exam Prep series is designed to help you pass your exams. Editors at MznLnx review your textbooks and then prepare these practice exams to help you master the textbook material. Unlike study guides, workbooks, and practice tests provided by the texbook publisher and textbook authors, *MznLnx* gives you **all** of the material in each chapter in exam form, not just samples, so you can be sure to nail your exam.

MECHANICAL

The MznLnx Exam Prep series creates exams that will help you learn the subject matter as well as test you on your understanding. Each question is designed to help you master the concept. Just working through the exams, you gain an understanding of the subject--its a simple mechanical process that produces success.

INTEGRATED STUDY GUIDE AND REVIEW

MznLnx is not just a set of exams designed to test you, its also a comprehensive review of the subject content. Each exam question is also a review of the concept, making sure that you will get the answer correct without having to go to other sources of material. You learn as you go! Its the easiest way to pass an exam.

HUMOR

Studying can be tedious and dry. MznLnx's instructional design includes moderate humor within the exam questions on occassion, to break the tedium and revitalize the brain

Chapter 1. Introduction to Algebraic Expressions 1

1. In mathematics, the word _____ is a term for any well-formed combination of mathematical symbols. For example,

    $x^2 + 3x - 4$

is an _____, while

)x) / 0

is not, because the parentheses are not balanced and division by zero is undefined.

Being an _____ is a syntactic concept - the meaning of the variables is irrelevant, but different fields have different notions of validity.â€¢See formal language for how _____s are constructed, and formal semantics for meaning.

   a. Arity
   b. Orthogonal
   c. Unit ring
   d. Expression

2. In mathematics, the _____ of a number n is the number that, when added to n, yields zero. The _____ of F is denoted −F.

For example, the _____ of 7 is −7, because 7 + (−7) = 0, and the _____ of −0.3 is 0.3, because −0.3 + 0.3 = 0.

   a. Isomorphism class
   b. Artinian ideal
   c. Additive inverse
   d. Interior algebra

3. A _____ is a symbol that stands for a value that may vary; the term usually occurs in opposition to constant, which is a symbol for a non-varying value, i.e. completely fixed or fixed in the context of use. The concepts of constants and _____s are fundamental to all modern mathematics, science, engineering, and computer programming.

Much of the basic theory for which we use _____s today, such as school geometry and algebra, was developed thousands of years ago, but the use of symbolic formulae and _____s is only several hundreds of years old.

a. -module
b. -equivalence
c. 2-bridge knot
d. Variable

4. A _____ is one of the basic shapes of geometry: a polygon with three corners or vertices and three sides or edges which are line segments. A _____ with vertices A, B, and C is denoted ABC.

In Euclidean geometry any three non-collinear points determine a unique _____ and a unique plane (i.e. a two-dimensional Euclidean space.)

a. 2-bridge knot
b. -module
c. -equivalence
d. Triangle

5. In geometry, a _____ is a quadrilateral with two sets of parallel sides. The opposite or facing sides of a _____ are of equal length, and the opposite angles of a _____ are of equal size. The three-dimensional counterpart of a _____ is a parallelepiped.
a. -equivalence
b. 2-bridge knot
c. -module
d. Parallelogram

6. _____ is the mathematical process of putting things together. The plus sign '+' means that numbers are added together. For example, in the picture on the right, there are 3 + 2 apples--meaning three apples and two other apples--which is the same as five apples, since 3 + 2 = 5.
a. Abelian P-root group
b. AKS primality test
c. ADE classification
d. Addition

7. Formally, a binary operation ∗ on a set S is called associative if it satisfies the _____:

Chapter 1. Introduction to Algebraic Expressions 3

$$(x * y) * z = x * (y * z) \quad \text{for all } x, y, z \in S.$$
Using * to denote a binary operation performed on a set

$$(xy)z = x(yz) = xyz \quad \text{for all } x, y, z \in S.$$
An example of multiplicative associativity

The evaluation order does not affect the value of such expressions, and it can be shown that the same holds for expressions containing any number of ∗ operations. Thus, when ∗ is associative, the evaluation order can therefore be left unspecified without causing ambiguity, by omitting the parentheses and writing simply:

xyz,

However, it is important to remember that changing the order of operations does not involve or permit changing the actual operations themselves by moving the operands around within the expression.

A very different perspective is obtained by rephrasing associativity using functional notation: f(f(x,y),z) = f(x,f(y,z)): when expressed in this form, associativity becomes less obvious.

a. Associative law
b. AKS primality test
c. ADE classification
d. Abelian P-root group

8. In mathematics, and in particular in abstract algebra, distributivity is a property of binary operations that generalises the _____ from elementary algebra. For example: <_____>
2 × (1 + 3) = (2 × 1) + (2 × 3.)

In the left-hand side of the above equation, the 2 multiplies the sum of 1 and 3; on the right-hand side, it multiplies the 1 and the 3 individually, with the results added afterwards.

a. -equivalence
b. -module
c. Distributive law
d. 2-bridge knot

9. In mathematics, _____ or factoring is the decomposition of an object ' href='/wiki/Matrix_(mathematics)'>matrix) into a product of other objects, or factors, which when multiplied together give the original. For example, the number 15 factors into primes as 3 × 5, and the polynomial x^2 − 4 factors as (x − 2)(x + 2.) In all cases, a product of simpler objects is obtained.

a. -module
b. 2-bridge knot
c. -equivalence
d. Factorization

10. A _____ is a three-dimensional solid object bounded by six square faces, facets or sides, with three meeting at each vertex. The _____ can also be called a regular hexahedron and is one of the five Platonic solids. It is a special kind of square prism, of rectangular parallelepiped and of trigonal trapezohedron.
a. 2-bridge knot
b. -equivalence
c. -module
d. Cube

11. In mathematics, especially in elementary arithmetic, _____ is an arithmetic operation which is the inverse of multiplication.

Specifically, if c times b equals a, written:

$$c \times b = a$$

where b is not zero, then a divided by b equals c, written:

$$\frac{a}{b} = c$$

For instance,

$$\frac{6}{3} = 2$$

since

$$2 \times 3 = 6.$$

In the above expression, a is called the dividend, b the divisor and c the quotient.

a. 2-bridge knot
b. Division
c. -module
d. -equivalence

12. In mathematics, a _____ or reciprocal for a number x, denoted by $\frac{1}{x}$ or x^{-1}, is a number which when multiplied by x yields the multiplicative identity, 1. The _____ of x is also called the reciprocal of x. The _____ of a fraction a/b is b/a.

a. 2-bridge knot
b. -equivalence
c. Multiplicative inverse
d. -module

13. In mathematics, a _____ is any number that can be expressed in the form

$$\frac{a}{b}, a, b \in \mathbb{Z}, b \neq 0$$

which says 'a divided by b, given that a and b are integers and b does not equal zero'. Since the denominator b may be equal to 1, every integer is a _____. The set of all _____s is denoted $\mathbb{Q}$ (for quotient.)

a. Ratio
b. Number system
c. -equivalence
d. Rational number

14. In elementary algebra, a _____ is a polynomial consisting of three terms; in other words, a _____ is the sum of three monomials. It can be factored using simple steps.

In linguistics, a _____ is a fixed expression which is made from three words; e.g. 'lights, camera, action', 'signed, sealed, delivered'.

a. Polynomial Diophantine equation
b. Hall polynomials
c. Finitary operation
d. Trinomial

15. _____ is one of the four basic arithmetic operations; it is the inverse of addition, meaning that if we start with any number and add any number and then subtract the same number we added, we return to the number we started with. _____ is denoted by a minus sign in infix notation.

The traditional names for the parts of the formula

$$c - b = a$$

are minuend (c) − subtrahend (b) = difference (a.)

   a. Subtraction
   b. -module
   c. 2-bridge knot
   d. -equivalence

16. The _____ are natural numbers including 0 ' href='/wiki/0_(number)'>0, 1, 2, 3, ...) and their negatives (0, −1, −2, −3, ...). They are numbers that can be written without a fractional or decimal component, and fall within the set {...
   a. Abelian P-root group
   b. AKS primality test
   c. ADE classification
   d. Integers

17. A _____ is an expression which compares quantities relative to each other. The most common examples involve two quantities, but in theory any number of quantities can be compared. In mathematical terms, they are represented by separating each quantity with a colon, for example the _____ 2:3, which is read as the _____ 'two to three'.
   a. Number system
   b. -equivalence
   c. Rational number
   d. Ratio

18. In geometry, a _____ is a straight curve. When geometry is used to model the real world, _____s are used to represent straight objects with negligible width and height. _____s are an idealisation of such objects and have no width or height at all and are usually considered to be infinitely long.
   a. Line
   b. 2-bridge knot
   c. -module
   d. -equivalence

Chapter 1. Introduction to Algebraic Expressions   7

19. In group theory, a branch of mathematics, the term _____ is used in two closely related senses:

    - the _____ of a group is its cardinality, i.e. the number of its elements;
    - the _____, sometimes period, of an element a of a group is the smallest positive integer m such that a^m = e (where e denotes the identity element of the group, and a^m denotes the product of m copies of a.) If no such m exists, we say that a has infinite _____. All elements of finite groups have finite _____.

    We denote the _____ of a group G by ord(G) or $|G|$ and the _____ of an element a by ord(a) or $|a|$.

    Example. The symmetric group S_3 has the following multiplication table.

    This group has six elements, so ord(S_3) = 6.

    a. Artin group
    b. Outer automorphism group
    c. Index calculus algorithm
    d. Order

20. In linear algebra, two n-by-n matrices A and B are called _____ if

    $$B = P^{-1}AP$$

    for some invertible n-by-n matrix P. _____ matrices represent the same linear transformation under two different bases, with P being the change of basis matrix.

    The matrix P is sometimes called a similarity transformation. In the context of matrix groups, similarity is sometimes referred to as conjugacy, with _____ matrices being conjugate.

    a. Skew-symmetric
    b. Zero matrix
    c. Cartan matrix
    d. Similar

21. In mathematics, more precisely in algebra, an _____ is a quantity that is not known, and cannot be solved for. An _____ is different from a variable, which is solvable, at least conditionally, from a given equation or set of equations. To make this distinction in an example, compare these two situations.

Chapter 1. Introduction to Algebraic Expressions

   a. Inverse element
   b. Indeterminate
   c. Algebraic function
   d. Anyonic Lie algebra

22. In technical applications of 3D computer graphics (CAx) such as computer-aided design and computer-aided manufacturing, _____s are one way of representing objects. The other ways are wireframe (lines and curves) and solids. Point clouds are also sometimes used as temporary ways to represent an object, with the goal of using the points to create one or more of the three permanent representations.
   a. 2-bridge knot
   b. Surface
   c. -equivalence
   d. -module

23. In its simplest meaning in mathematics and logic, an _____ is an action or procedure which produces a new value from one or more input values. There are two common types of _____s: unary and binary. Unary _____s involve only one value, such as negation and trigonometric functions.
   a. Operation
   b. ADE classification
   c. Abelian P-root group
   d. AKS primality test

24. In algebra and computer programming, when a number or expression is both preceded and followed by an operator such as minus or times, a rule is needed to specify which operator should be applied first; this rule is known as a _____, or more informally order of operation. From the earliest use of mathematical notation, multiplication took precedence over addition, whichever side of a number it appeared on. Thus 3 + 4 × 5 = 5 × 4 + 3 = 23.
   a. Precedence rule
   b. Planar ternary ring
   c. Formal power series
   d. Setoid

Chapter 2. Equations, Inequalities, and Problem Solving

1. In mathematics, a _____ is a constant multiplicative factor of a certain object. For example, in the expression $9x^2$, the _____ of x^2 is 9.

The object can be such things as a variable, a vector, a function, etc.

a. Tschirnhaus transformation
b. Constant term
c. Coefficient
d. Vandermonde polynomial

2. _____ is the mathematical process of putting things together. The plus sign '+' means that numbers are added together. For example, in the picture on the right, there are 3 + 2 apples--meaning three apples and two other apples--which is the same as five apples, since 3 + 2 = 5.

a. ADE classification
b. AKS primality test
c. Abelian P-root group
d. Addition

3. In mathematics, the word _____ is a term for any well-formed combination of mathematical symbols. For example,

$$x^2 + 3x - 4$$

is an _____, while

$$)x) / 0$$

is not, because the parentheses are not balanced and division by zero is undefined.

Being an _____ is a syntactic concept - the meaning of the variables is irrelevant, but different fields have different notions of validity.â€¢See formal language for how _____s are constructed, and formal semantics for meaning.

a. Unit ring
b. Orthogonal
c. Arity
d. Expression

4. A _____ is a three-dimensional solid object bounded by six square faces, facets or sides, with three meeting at each vertex. The _____ can also be called a regular hexahedron and is one of the five Platonic solids. It is a special kind of square prism, of rectangular parallelepiped and of trigonal trapezohedron.

a. Cube
b. -equivalence
c. -module
d. 2-bridge knot

5. In technical applications of 3D computer graphics (CAx) such as computer-aided design and computer-aided manufacturing, _____s are one way of representing objects. The other ways are wireframe (lines and curves) and solids. Point clouds are also sometimes used as temporary ways to represent an object, with the goal of using the points to create one or more of the three permanent representations.
   a. Surface
   b. -equivalence
   c. 2-bridge knot
   d. -module

6. In mathematics, the term _____ is used to describe an algebraic structures which in some sense cannot be divided by a smaller structure of the same type. Put another way, an algebraic structure is _____ if the kernel of every homomorphism is either the whole structure or a single element. Some examples are:

   - A group is called a _____ group if it does not contain a non-trivial proper normal subgroup.
   - A ring is called a _____ ring if it does not contain a non-trivial two sided ideal.
   - A module is called a _____ module if does not contain a non-trivial submodule.
   - An algebra is called a _____ algebra if does not contain a non-trivial two sided ideal.

   The general pattern is that the structure admits no non-trivial congruence relations.

   a. Commutativity
   b. Polarization identity
   c. Linear combinations
   d. Simple

7. In mathematics, specifically group theory, the _____ of a subgroup H in a group G is the e;relative sizee; of H in G. For example, if H has _____ 2 in G, then intuitively e;halfe; of the elements of G lie in H. The _____ of H in G is usually denoted $|G:H|$ or $[G:H]$.

   If G and H are finite groups, then the _____ of H in G is simply the quotient of the orders of the two groups:

   $$|G:H| = \frac{|G|}{|H|}.$$

Chapter 2. Equations, Inequalities, and Problem Solving

By Lagrange's theorem, this number is always a positive integer.

If G and H are infinite, then the _____ of H is G is defined as the number of cosets of H in G.

- a. Outer automorphism
- b. Index
- c. Inner automorphism
- d. Even permutations

8. In mathematics, _____(F_n) is the _____er automorphism group of a free group on n generators. These groups play an important role in geometric group theory.

_____(F_n) acts geometrically on a cell complex known as _____er space, which can be thought of as the Teichmüller space for a bouquet of circles.

- a. Abelian P-root group
- b. AKS primality test
- c. ADE classification
- d. Out

9. In geometry and trigonometry, an _____ is the figure formed by two rays sharing a common endpoint, called the vertex of the _____. The magnitude of the _____ is the 'amount of rotation' that separates the two rays, and can be measured by considering the length of circular arc swept out when one ray is rotated about the vertex to coincide with the other Where there is no possibility of confusion, the term '_____' is used interchangeably for both the geometric configuration itself and for its angular magnitude (which is simply a numerical quantity.)

- a. ADE classification
- b. Angle
- c. Abelian P-root group
- d. AKS primality test

10. A _____ is a symbol that stands for a value that may vary; the term usually occurs in opposition to constant, which is a symbol for a non-varying value, i.e. completely fixed or fixed in the context of use. The concepts of constants and _____s are fundamental to all modern mathematics, science, engineering, and computer programming.

Much of the basic theory for which we use _____s today, such as school geometry and algebra, was developed thousands of years ago, but the use of symbolic formulae and _____s is only several hundreds of years old.

a. -equivalence
b. -module
c. Variable
d. 2-bridge knot

Chapter 3. Introduction to Graphing

1. In geometry, a _____ is a straight curve. When geometry is used to model the real world, _____s are used to represent straight objects with negligible width and height. _____s are an idealisation of such objects and have no width or height at all and are usually considered to be infinitely long.
    a. -module
    b. Line
    c. 2-bridge knot
    d. -equivalence

2. In mathematics, the _____ of a vector space V is the cardinality (i.e. the number of vectors) of a basis of V. It is sometimes called Hamel _____ or algebraic _____ to distinguish it from other types of _____. All bases of a vector space have equal cardinality and so the _____ of a vector space is uniquely defined. The _____ of the vector space V over the field F can be written as $\dim_F(V)$ or as [V : F], read '_____ of V over F'.
    a. Dual basis
    b. Dimension
    c. Partial trace
    d. Cofactor

3. In mathematics, a (B, N) _____ is a structure on groups of Lie type that allows one to give uniform proofs of many results, instead of giving a large number of case-by-case proofs. Roughly speaking, it shows that all such groups are similar to the general linear group over a field. They were invented by the mathematician Jacques Tits, and are also sometimes known as Tits systems.
    a. Group representations
    b. Rank of a group
    c. Group action
    d. Pair

4. In mathematics, a _____ is a flat surface. _____s can arise as subspaces of some higher dimensional space, as with the walls of a room, or they may enjoy an independent existence in their own right, as in the setting of Euclidean geometry
    a. -equivalence
    b. Plane
    c. Similarity
    d. -module

5. A _____ is a symbol that stands for a value that may vary; the term usually occurs in opposition to constant, which is a symbol for a non-varying value, i.e. completely fixed or fixed in the context of use. The concepts of constants and _____s are fundamental to all modern mathematics, science, engineering, and computer programming.

14   *Chapter 3. Introduction to Graphing*

Much of the basic theory for which we use _____s today, such as school geometry and algebra, was developed thousands of years ago, but the use of symbolic formulae and _____s is only several hundreds of years old.

   a. 2-bridge knot
   b. -equivalence
   c. Variable
   d. -module

6. In geometry, two lines or planes (or a line and a plane), are considered _____ to each other if they form congruent adjacent angles (an L-shape.) The term may be used as a noun or adjective. Thus, referring to Figure 1, the line AB is the _____ to CD through the point B. Note that by definition, a line is infinitely long, and strictly speaking AB and CD in this example represent line segments of two infinitely long lines.
   a. -module
   b. -equivalence
   c. Perpendicular
   d. 2-bridge knot

Chapter 4. Polynomials

1. _____ is the mathematical process of putting things together. The plus sign '+' means that numbers are added together. For example, in the picture on the right, there are 3 + 2 apples--meaning three apples and two other apples--which is the same as five apples, since 3 + 2 = 5.

   a. ADE classification
   b. Abelian P-root group
   c. AKS primality test
   d. Addition

2. Formally, a binary operation $*$ on a set S is called associative if it satisfies the _____:

$$(x * y) * z = x * (y * z) \quad \text{for all } x, y, z \in S.$$

Using * to denote a binary operation performed on a set

$$(xy)z = x(yz) = xyz \quad \text{for all } x, y, z \in S.$$

An example of multiplicative associativity

The evaluation order does not affect the value of such expressions, and it can be shown that the same holds for expressions containing any number of $*$ operations. Thus, when $*$ is associative, the evaluation order can therefore be left unspecified without causing ambiguity, by omitting the parentheses and writing simply:

xyz,

However, it is important to remember that changing the order of operations does not involve or permit changing the actual operations themselves by moving the operands around within the expression.

A very different perspective is obtained by rephrasing associativity using functional notation: f(f(x,y),z) = f(x,f(y,z)): when expressed in this form, associativity becomes less obvious.

   a. Abelian P-root group
   b. AKS primality test
   c. ADE classification
   d. Associative law

3. In mathematics, especially in elementary arithmetic, _____ is an arithmetic operation which is the inverse of multiplication.

Specifically, if c times b equals a, written:

$$c \times b = a$$

Chapter 4. Polynomials

where b is not zero, then a divided by b equals c, written:

$$\frac{a}{b} = c$$

For instance,

$$\frac{6}{3} = 2$$

since

$$2 \times 3 = 6.$$

In the above expression, a is called the dividend, b the divisor and c the quotient.

  a. 2-bridge knot
  b. -module
  c. -equivalence
  d. Division

4. _____ is one of the four basic arithmetic operations; it is the inverse of addition, meaning that if we start with any number and add any number and then subtract the same number we added, we return to the number we started with. _____ is denoted by a minus sign in infix notation.

The traditional names for the parts of the formula

  c − b = a

are minuend (c) − subtrahend (b) = difference (a.)

  a. -module
  b. 2-bridge knot
  c. -equivalence
  d. Subtraction

5. In mathematics, the _____ of a number n is the number that, when added to n, yields zero. The _____ of F is denoted −F.

For example, the _____ of 7 is −7, because 7 + (−7) = 0, and the _____ of −0.3 is 0.3, because −0.3 + 0.3 = 0.

   a. Interior algebra
   b. Artinian ideal
   c. Additive inverse
   d. Isomorphism class

6. In mathematics, the word _____ means two different things in the context of polynomials:

   - The first meaning is a product of powers of variables, or formally any value obtained from 1 by finitely many multiplications by a variable. If only a single variable x is considered this means that any _____ is either 1 or a power x^n of x, with n a positive integer. If several variables are considered, say, x, y, z, then each can be given an exponent, so that any _____ is of the form $x^a y^b z^c$ with a,b,c nonnegative integers (taking note that any exponent 0 makes the corresponding factor equal to 1.)
   - The second meaning of _____ includes _____ s in the first sense, but also allows multiplication by any constant, so that − $7x^5$ and $(3 − 4i)x^4 yz^{13}$ are also considered to be _____ s (the second example assuming polynomials in x, y, z over the complex numbers are considered.)

With either definition, the set of _____ s is a subset of all polynomials that is closed under multiplication.

Both uses of this notion can be found, and in many cases the distinction is simply ignored, see for instance examples for the first and second meaning, and an unclear definition. In informal discussions the distinction is seldom important, and tendency is towards the broader second meaning. When studying the structure of polynomials however, one often definitely needs a notion with the first meaning.

   a. Power sum symmetric polynomial
   b. Diagonal form
   c. Schur polynomials
   d. Monomial

Chapter 4. Polynomials

7. In elementary algebra, a _____ is a polynomial with two terms--the sum of two monomials--often bound by parenthesis or brackets when operated upon. It is the simplest kind of polynomial other than monomials.

- The _____ $a^2 - b^2$ can be factored as the product of two other _____s:

  $a^2 - b^2 = (a + b)(a - b.)$

  This is a special case of the more general formula: $a^{n+1} - b^{n+1} = (a - b) \sum_{k=0}^{n} a^k b^{n-k}$.

- The product of a pair of linear _____s (ax + b) and (cx + d) is:

  $(ax + b)(cx + d) = acx^2 + axd + bcx + bd.$

- A _____ raised to the nth power, represented as

  $(a + b)^n$

  can be expanded by means of the _____ theorem or, equivalently, using Pascal's triangle. Taking a simple example, the perfect square _____ $(p + q)^2$ can be found by squaring the :first digit, adding twice the product of the first and second digit and finally adding the square of the second digit, to give $p^2 + 2pq + q^2$.

  a. Theory of equations
  b. Content
  c. Binomial
  d. Generalized arithmetic progression

8. In mathematics, a _____ is a constant multiplicative factor of a certain object. For example, in the expression $9x^2$, the _____ of x^2 is 9.

The object can be such things as a variable, a vector, a function, etc.

  a. Tschirnhaus transformation
  b. Constant term
  c. Coefficient
  d. Vandermonde polynomial

9. In mathematics, there are several meanings of _____ depending on the subject.

A _____, usually denoted by ° (the _____ symbol), is a measurement of plane angle, representing $1/360$ of a full rotation. When that angle is with respect to a reference meridian, it indicates a location along a great circle of a sphere, such as Earth , Mars, or the celestial sphere.

a. Symmetric difference
b. Relation algebra
c. Median algebra
d. Degree

10. When a polynomial is expressed as a sum or difference of terms (e.g., in standard or canonical form), the exponent of the term with the highest exponent is the _____. The degree of a term is the sum of the powers of each variable in the term. The words degree and order are used interchangeably.

   a. Multivariate division algorithm
   b. Secondary polynomials
   c. Lommel polynomial
   d. Degree of the polynomial

11. In elementary algebra, a _____ is a polynomial consisting of three terms; in other words, a _____ is the sum of three monomials. It can be factored using simple steps.

In linguistics, a _____ is a fixed expression which is made from three words; e.g. 'lights, camera, action', 'signed, sealed, delivered'.

   a. Finitary operation
   b. Hall polynomials
   c. Polynomial Diophantine equation
   d. Trinomial

12. In mathematics, and in particular in abstract algebra, distributivity is a property of binary operations that generalises the _____ from elementary algebra. For example: <_____>
   2 × (1 + 3) = (2 × 1) + (2 × 3.)

In the left-hand side of the above equation, the 2 multiplies the sum of 1 and 3; on the right-hand side, it multiplies the 1 and the 3 individually, with the results added afterwards.

   a. -equivalence
   b. Distributive law
   c. 2-bridge knot
   d. -module

13. In linear algebra, two n-by-n matrices A and B are called _____ if

$$B = P^{-1}AP$$

for some invertible n-by-n matrix P. _____ matrices represent the same linear transformation under two different bases, with P being the change of basis matrix.

The matrix P is sometimes called a similarity transformation. In the context of matrix groups, similarity is sometimes referred to as conjugacy, with _____ matrices being conjugate.

- a. Cartan matrix
- b. Skew-symmetric
- c. Similar
- d. Zero matrix

14. In group theory, a branch of mathematics, the term _____ is used in two closely related senses:

   - the _____ of a group is its cardinality, i.e. the number of its elements;
   - the _____, sometimes period, of an element a of a group is the smallest positive integer m such that $a^m = e$ (where e denotes the identity element of the group, and a^m denotes the product of m copies of a.) If no such m exists, we say that a has infinite _____. All elements of finite groups have finite _____.

   We denote the _____ of a group G by ord(G) or $|G|$ and the _____ of an element a by ord(a) or $|a|$.

   Example. The symmetric group S_3 has the following multiplication table.

   This group has six elements, so ord(S_3) = 6.

   - a. Outer automorphism group
   - b. Order
   - c. Artin group
   - d. Index calculus algorithm

15. In mathematics, the word _____ is a term for any well-formed combination of mathematical symbols. For example,

   $x^2 + 3x - 4$

is an _____, while

)x) / 0

is not, because the parentheses are not balanced and division by zero is undefined.

Being an _____ is a syntactic concept - the meaning of the variables is irrelevant, but different fields have different notions of validity.â€See formal language for how _____s are constructed, and formal semantics for meaning.

- a. Arity
- b. Expression
- c. Orthogonal
- d. Unit ring

16. In linear algebra, the _____ of an n-by-n square matrix A is defined to be the sum of the elements on the main diagonal (the diagonal from the upper left to the lower right) of A, i.e.,

$$\operatorname{tr}(A) = a_{11} + a_{22} + \cdots + a_{nn} = \sum_{i=1}^{n} a_{ii}$$

where a_{ij} represents the entry on the ith row and jth column of A. Equivalently, the _____ of a matrix is the sum of its eigenvalues, making it an invariant with respect to a change of basis. This characterization can be used to define the _____ for a linear operator in general.

Note that the _____ is only defined for a square matrix (i.e. n×n.)

- a. Defective matrix
- b. Trace
- c. Coefficient matrix
- d. Dot product

17. In technical applications of 3D computer graphics (CAx) such as computer-aided design and computer-aided manufacturing, _____s are one way of representing objects. The other ways are wireframe (lines and curves) and solids. Point clouds are also sometimes used as temporary ways to represent an object, with the goal of using the points to create one or more of the three permanent representations.

Chapter 4. Polynomials

   a. 2-bridge knot
   b. -module
   c. -equivalence
   d. Surface

18. A _____ is a symbol that stands for a value that may vary; the term usually occurs in opposition to constant, which is a symbol for a non-varying value, i.e. completely fixed or fixed in the context of use. The concepts of constants and _____s are fundamental to all modern mathematics, science, engineering, and computer programming.

Much of the basic theory for which we use _____s today, such as school geometry and algebra, was developed thousands of years ago, but the use of symbolic formulae and _____s is only several hundreds of years old.

   a. Variable
   b. -module
   c. -equivalence
   d. 2-bridge knot

19. In algebraic geometry, _____s are a generalization of codimension one subvarieties of algebraic varieties; two different generalizations are in common use, Cartier _____s and Weil _____s The concepts agree on non-singular varieties over algebraically closed fields.

A Weil _____ is a locally finite linear combination (with integral coefficients) of irreducible subvarieties of codimension one.

   a. Divisor
   b. Picard group
   c. Lefschetz pencil
   d. Linear system of divisors

Chapter 5. Polynomials and Factoring

1. In mathematics, _____ or factoring is the decomposition of an object ' href='/wiki/Matrix_(mathematics)'>matrix) into a product of other objects, or factors, which when multiplied together give the original. For example, the number 15 factors into primes as 3 × 5, and the polynomial $x^2 - 4$ factors as $(x - 2)(x + 2)$. In all cases, a product of simpler objects is obtained.
    a. Factorization
    b. -equivalence
    c. -module
    d. 2-bridge knot

2. In mathematics, the word _____ is a term for any well-formed combination of mathematical symbols. For example,

    $$x^2 + 3x - 4$$

    is an _____, while

    $$)x) / 0$$

    is not, because the parentheses are not balanced and division by zero is undefined.

    Being an _____ is a syntactic concept - the meaning of the variables is irrelevant, but different fields have different notions of validity.â€¢See formal language for how _____s are constructed, and formal semantics for meaning.

    a. Orthogonal
    b. Arity
    c. Unit ring
    d. Expression

3. In elementary algebra, a _____ is a polynomial consisting of three terms; in other words, a _____ is the sum of three monomials. It can be factored using simple steps.

    In linguistics, a _____ is a fixed expression which is made from three words; e.g. 'lights, camera, action', 'signed, sealed, delivered'.

    a. Polynomial Diophantine equation
    b. Hall polynomials
    c. Trinomial
    d. Finitary operation

Chapter 5. Polynomials and Factoring

4. In elementary algebra, a _____ is a polynomial with two terms--the sum of two monomials--often bound by parenthesis or brackets when operated upon. It is the simplest kind of polynomial other than monomials.

- The _____ $a^2 - b^2$ can be factored as the product of two other _____ s:

    $a^2 - b^2 = (a + b)(a - b.)$

    This is a special case of the more general formula:
    $$a^{n+1} - b^{n+1} = (a - b) \sum_{k=0}^{n} a^k b^{n-k}$$

- The product of a pair of linear _____ s (ax + b) and (cx + d) is:

    $(ax + b)(cx + d) = acx^2 + axd + bcx + bd.$

- A _____ raised to the nth power, represented as

    $(a + b)^n$

    can be expanded by means of the _____ theorem or, equivalently, using Pascal's triangle. Taking a simple example, the perfect square _____ $(p + q)^2$ can be found by squaring the :first digit, adding twice the product of the first and second digit and finally adding the square of the second digit, to give $p^2 + 2pq + q^2$.

    a. Generalized arithmetic progression
    b. Content
    c. Theory of equations
    d. Binomial

5. In mathematics, a _____ is a polynomial equation of the second degree. The general form is

    $$ax^2 + bx + c = 0$$

The quadratic coefficient a is the coefficient of x^2, the linear coefficient b is the coefficient of x, and c is the constant coefficient, also called the free term or constant term.

_____ s are called quadratic because the variable in the leading term is squared.

a. Quadratic equation
b. Rationalisation
c. Cubic function
d. Difference of two squares

Chapter 5. Polynomials and Factoring

6. _____ is the mathematical process of putting things together. The plus sign '+' means that numbers are added together. For example, in the picture on the right, there are 3 + 2 apples--meaning three apples and two other apples--which is the same as five apples, since 3 + 2 = 5.

   a. AKS primality test
   b. Abelian P-root group
   c. ADE classification
   d. Addition

7. In mathematics, a _____ of a number x is any number which, when repeatedly multiplied by itself, eventually yields x:

$$r \times r \times \cdots \times r = x.$$

In terms of exponentiation, r is a _____ of x if

$$r^n = x$$

for some positive integer n. For example, 2 is a _____ of 16 since $2^4 = 2 \times 2 \times 2 \times 2 = 16$.

The number n is called the degree of the _____.

   a. Rationalisation
   b. Difference of two squares
   c. Cubic function
   d. Root

8. In geometry and trigonometry, an _____ is the figure formed by two rays sharing a common endpoint, called the vertex of the _____ . The magnitude of the _____ is the 'amount of rotation' that separates the two rays, and can be measured by considering the length of circular arc swept out when one ray is rotated about the vertex to coincide with the other Where there is no possibility of confusion, the term '_____' is used interchangeably for both the geometric configuration itself and for its angular magnitude (which is simply a numerical quantity.)

   a. Angle
   b. Abelian P-root group
   c. ADE classification
   d. AKS primality test

9. A _____ is a triangle in which one angle is a right angle.

The side opposite the right angle is called the hypotenuse (side [BC] in the figure below.) In addition, the sides adjacent to the right angle are called legs or catheti (singular: cathetus.)

   a. Right triangle
   b. -equivalence
   c. 2-bridge knot
   d. -module

10. A _____ is one of the basic shapes of geometry: a polygon with three corners or vertices and three sides or edges which are line segments. A _____ with vertices A, B, and C is denoted ABC.

In Euclidean geometry any three non-collinear points determine a unique _____ and a unique plane (i.e. a two-dimensional Euclidean space.)

   a. -equivalence
   b. -module
   c. Triangle
   d. 2-bridge knot

Chapter 6. Rational Expressions and Equations

1. In mathematics, a _____ is any number that can be expressed in the form

    $$\frac{a}{b}, a, b \in \mathbb{Z}, b \neq 0$$

    which says 'a divided by b, given that a and b are integers and b does not equal zero'. Since the denominator b may be equal to 1, every integer is a _____. The set of all _____s is denoted $\mathbb{Q}$ (for quotient.)

    a. -equivalence
    b. Ratio
    c. Number system
    d. Rational number

2. _____ is the mathematical process of putting things together. The plus sign '+' means that numbers are added together. For example, in the picture on the right, there are 3 + 2 apples--meaning three apples and two other apples--which is the same as five apples, since 3 + 2 = 5.
    a. ADE classification
    b. AKS primality test
    c. Abelian P-root group
    d. Addition

3. In mathematics, the word _____ is a term for any well-formed combination of mathematical symbols. For example,

    $x^2 + 3x - 4$

    is an _____, while

)x) / 0

    is not, because the parentheses are not balanced and division by zero is undefined.

    Being an _____ is a syntactic concept - the meaning of the variables is irrelevant, but different fields have different notions of validity.â€¢See formal language for how _____s are constructed, and formal semantics for meaning.

    a. Unit ring
    b. Orthogonal
    c. Arity
    d. Expression

Chapter 6. Rational Expressions and Equations

4. In mathematics, the _____ of a number n is the number that, when added to n, yields zero. The _____ of F is denoted −F.

   For example, the _____ of 7 is −7, because 7 + (−7) = 0, and the _____ of −0.3 is 0.3, because −0.3 + 0.3 = 0.

   a. Artinian ideal
   b. Interior algebra
   c. Isomorphism class
   d. Additive inverse

5. Formally, a binary operation ∗ on a set S is called associative if it satisfies the _____:

   $$(x * y) * z = x * (y * z) \quad \text{for all } x, y, z \in S.$$
   Using * to denote a binary operation performed on a set

   $$(xy)z = x(yz) = xyz \quad \text{for all } x, y, z \in S.$$
   An example of multiplicative associativity

   The evaluation order does not affect the value of such expressions, and it can be shown that the same holds for expressions containing any number of ∗ operations. Thus, when ∗ is associative, the evaluation order can therefore be left unspecified without causing ambiguity, by omitting the parentheses and writing simply:

   xyz,

   However, it is important to remember that changing the order of operations does not involve or permit changing the actual operations themselves by moving the operands around within the expression.

   A very different perspective is obtained by rephrasing associativity using functional notation: f(f(x,y),z) = f(x,f(y,z)): when expressed in this form, associativity becomes less obvious.

   a. ADE classification
   b. Abelian P-root group
   c. Associative law
   d. AKS primality test

6. In mathematics, especially in elementary arithmetic, _____ is an arithmetic operation which is the inverse of multiplication.

Chapter 6. Rational Expressions and Equations

Specifically, if c times b equals a, written:

$$c \times b = a$$

where b is not zero, then a divided by b equals c, written:

$$\frac{a}{b} = c$$

For instance,

$$\frac{6}{3} = 2$$

since

$$2 \times 3 = 6.$$

In the above expression, a is called the dividend, b the divisor and c the quotient.

    a. 2-bridge knot
    b. -equivalence
    c. -module
    d. Division

7. _____ is one of the four basic arithmetic operations; it is the inverse of addition, meaning that if we start with any number and add any number and then subtract the same number we added, we return to the number we started with. _____ is denoted by a minus sign in infix notation.

The traditional names for the parts of the formula

    c − b = a

are minuend (c) − subtrahend (b) = difference (a.)

    a. 2-bridge knot
    b. -equivalence
    c. Subtraction
    d. -module

Chapter 6. Rational Expressions and Equations

8. In mathematics, _____ or factoring is the decomposition of an object ' href='/wiki/Matrix_(mathematics)'>matrix) into a product of other objects, or factors, which when multiplied together give the original. For example, the number 15 factors into primes as 3 × 5, and the polynomial $x^2 - 4$ factors as $(x - 2)(x + 2)$. In all cases, a product of simpler objects is obtained.
   a. -module
   b. 2-bridge knot
   c. -equivalence
   d. Factorization

9. A _____ is an expression which compares quantities relative to each other. The most common examples involve two quantities, but in theory any number of quantities can be compared. In mathematical terms, they are represented by separating each quantity with a colon, for example the _____ 2:3, which is read as the _____ 'two to three'.
   a. -equivalence
   b. Rational number
   c. Number system
   d. Ratio

10. In linear algebra, two n-by-n matrices A and B are called _____ if

$$B = P^{-1}AP$$

for some invertible n-by-n matrix P. _____ matrices represent the same linear transformation under two different bases, with P being the change of basis matrix.

The matrix P is sometimes called a similarity transformation. In the context of matrix groups, similarity is sometimes referred to as conjugacy, with _____ matrices being conjugate.

   a. Skew-symmetric
   b. Cartan matrix
   c. Zero matrix
   d. Similar

11. A _____ is one of the basic shapes of geometry: a polygon with three corners or vertices and three sides or edges which are line segments. A _____ with vertices A, B, and C is denoted ABC.

In Euclidean geometry any three non-collinear points determine a unique _____ and a unique plane (i.e. a two-dimensional Euclidean space.)

a. -module
b. -equivalence
c. 2-bridge knot
d. Triangle

Chapter 7. Systems and More Graphing

1. In geometry, a _____ is a straight curve. When geometry is used to model the real world, _____s are used to represent straight objects with negligible width and height. _____s are an idealisation of such objects and have no width or height at all and are usually considered to be infinitely long.
   a. 2-bridge knot
   b. Line
   c. -equivalence
   d. -module

2. An _____ is an equation in a system of simultaneous equations which cannot be derived algebraically from the other equations.
   a. Eigendecomposition
   b. Orthogonalization
   c. Elementary matrix
   d. Independent equation

3. _____ is the mathematical process of putting things together. The plus sign '+' means that numbers are added together. For example, in the picture on the right, there are 3 + 2 apples--meaning three apples and two other apples--which is the same as five apples, since 3 + 2 = 5.
   a. Abelian P-root group
   b. ADE classification
   c. AKS primality test
   d. Addition

4. In mathematics, the word _____ is a term for any well-formed combination of mathematical symbols. For example,

   $x^2 + 3x - 4$

is an _____, while

   $)x) / 0$

is not, because the parentheses are not balanced and division by zero is undefined.

Being an _____ is a syntactic concept - the meaning of the variables is irrelevant, but different fields have different notions of validity.â€¢See formal language for how _____s are constructed, and formal semantics for meaning.

Chapter 7. Systems and More Graphing

   a. Expression
   b. Arity
   c. Unit ring
   d. Orthogonal

5. In mathematics, specifically group theory, the _____ of a subgroup H in a group G is the e;relative sizee; of H in G. For example, if H has _____ 2 in G, then intuitively e;halfe; of the elements of G lie in H. The _____ of H in G is usually denoted |G : H| or [G : H].

If G and H are finite groups, then the _____ of H in G is simply the quotient of the orders of the two groups:

$$|G : H| = \frac{|G|}{|H|}.$$

By Lagrange's theorem, this number is always a positive integer.

If G and H are infinite, then the _____ of H is G is defined as the number of cosets of H in G.

   a. Outer automorphism
   b. Inner automorphism
   c. Even permutations
   d. Index

6. A _____ is a symbol that stands for a value that may vary; the term usually occurs in opposition to constant, which is a symbol for a non-varying value, i.e. completely fixed or fixed in the context of use. The concepts of constants and _____ s are fundamental to all modern mathematics, science, engineering, and computer programming.

Much of the basic theory for which we use _____ s today, such as school geometry and algebra, was developed thousands of years ago, but the use of symbolic formulae and _____ s is only several hundreds of years old.

   a. 2-bridge knot
   b. -equivalence
   c. Variable
   d. -module

Chapter 8. Radical Expressions and Equations

1. The _____ of a Lie algebra 𝔤 is a particular ideal of 𝔤.

Let 𝔤 be a Lie algebra. The _____ of 𝔤 is defined as the largest solvable ideal of 𝔤.

   a. Garside element
   b. Cyclically reduced word
   c. Class sum
   d. Radical

2. In mathematics, a _____ of a number x is a number r such that r^2 = x, or, in other words, a number r whose square (the result of multiplying the number by itself) is x.

Every non-negative real number x has a unique non-negative _____, called the principal _____, which is denoted with a radical symbol as $\sqrt{x}$, or, using exponent notation, as $x^{1/2}$. For example, the principal _____ of 9 is 3, denoted $\sqrt{9} = 3$, because 3^2 = 3 × 3 = 9.

   a. 2-bridge knot
   b. -module
   c. -equivalence
   d. Square root

3. In mathematics, the _____ of a real number is its numerical value without regard to its sign. So, for example, 3 is the _____ of both 3 and −3.

The _____ of a number a is denoted by | a |.

   a. Abelian P-root group
   b. Absolute value
   c. ADE classification
   d. AKS primality test

4. In mathematics, the word _____ is a term for any well-formed combination of mathematical symbols. For example,

   $x^2 + 3x - 4$

is an _____, while

)x) / 0

is not, because the parentheses are not balanced and division by zero is undefined.

Being an _____ is a syntactic concept - the meaning of the variables is irrelevant, but different fields have different notions of validity.â€¢See formal language for how _____s are constructed, and formal semantics for meaning.

a. Orthogonal
b. Arity
c. Expression
d. Unit ring

5. In mathematics, a _____ of a number x is any number which, when repeatedly multiplied by itself, eventually yields x:

$$r \times r \times \cdots \times r = x.$$

In terms of exponentiation, r is a _____ of x if

$$r^n = x$$

for some positive integer n. For example, 2 is a _____ of 16 since $2^4 = 2 \times 2 \times 2 \times 2 = 16$.

The number n is called the degree of the _____.

a. Rationalisation
b. Difference of two squares
c. Cubic function
d. Root

6. Formally, a binary operation ∗ on a set S is called associative if it satisfies the _____:

$$(x * y) * z = x * (y * z) \qquad \text{for all } x, y, z \in S.$$

Using * to denote a binary operation performed on a set

$$(xy)z = x(yz) = xyz \qquad \text{for all } x, y, z \in S.$$

An example of multiplicative associativity

The evaluation order does not affect the value of such expressions, and it can be shown that the same holds for expressions containing any number of ∗ operations. Thus, when ∗ is associative, the evaluation order can therefore be left unspecified without causing ambiguity, by omitting the parentheses and writing simply:

xyz,

However, it is important to remember that changing the order of operations does not involve or permit changing the actual operations themselves by moving the operands around within the expression.

A very different perspective is obtained by rephrasing associativity using functional notation: f(f(x,y),z) = f(x,f(y,z)): when expressed in this form, associativity becomes less obvious.

a. Abelian P-root group
b. AKS primality test
c. Associative law
d. ADE classification

7. In mathematics, especially in elementary arithmetic, _____ is an arithmetic operation which is the inverse of multiplication.

Specifically, if c times b equals a, written:

$$c \times b = a$$

where b is not zero, then a divided by b equals c, written:

$$\frac{a}{b} = c$$

For instance,

$$\frac{6}{3} = 2$$

since

$$2 \times 3 = 6.$$

In the above expression, a is called the dividend, b the divisor and c the quotient.

Chapter 8. Radical Expressions and Equations

a. -equivalence
b. Division
c. 2-bridge knot
d. -module

8. _____ is the mathematical process of putting things together. The plus sign '+' means that numbers are added together. For example, in the picture on the right, there are 3 + 2 apples--meaning three apples and two other apples--which is the same as five apples, since 3 + 2 = 5.

a. Abelian P-root group
b. Addition
c. ADE classification
d. AKS primality test

9. _____ is one of the four basic arithmetic operations; it is the inverse of addition, meaning that if we start with any number and add any number and then subtract the same number we added, we return to the number we started with. _____ is denoted by a minus sign in infix notation.

The traditional names for the parts of the formula

$$c - b = a$$

are minuend (c) − subtrahend (b) = difference (a.)

a. Subtraction
b. 2-bridge knot
c. -equivalence
d. -module

10. In mathematics, the _____ of a number n is the number that, when added to n, yields zero. The _____ of F is denoted −F.

For example, the _____ of 7 is −7, because 7 + (−7) = 0, and the _____ of −0.3 is 0.3, because −0.3 + 0.3 = 0.

a. Interior algebra
b. Isomorphism class
c. Artinian ideal
d. Additive inverse

11. In algebra, a _____ of an element in a quadratic extension field of a field K is its image under the unique non-identity automorphism of the extended field that fixes K. If the extension is generated by a square root of an element r of K, then the _____ of $a + b\sqrt{r}$ is $a - b\sqrt{r}$ for $a, b \in K$, and in particular in the case of the field C of complex numbers as an extension of the field R of real numbers (where r = − 1), the complex _____ of a + bi is a − bi.

Forming the sum or product of any element of the extension field with its _____ always gives an element of K. This can be used to rewrite a quotient of numbers in the extended field so that the denominator lies in K, by multiplying numerator and denominator by the _____ of the denominator. This process is called rationalization of the denominator, in particular if K is the field Q of rational numbers.

   a. Field arithmetic
   b. Conjugate
   c. K-theory
   d. Digital root

12. A _____ is a triangle in which one angle is a right angle.

The side opposite the right angle is called the hypotenuse (side [BC] in the figure below.) In addition, the sides adjacent to the right angle are called legs or catheti (singular: cathetus.)

   a. 2-bridge knot
   b. Right triangle
   c. -equivalence
   d. -module

13. A _____ is one of the basic shapes of geometry: a polygon with three corners or vertices and three sides or edges which are line segments. A _____ with vertices A, B, and C is denoted ABC.

In Euclidean geometry any three non-collinear points determine a unique _____ and a unique plane (i.e. a two-dimensional Euclidean space.)

   a. -module
   b. Triangle
   c. -equivalence
   d. 2-bridge knot

14. A _____ is a three-dimensional solid object bounded by six square faces, facets or sides, with three meeting at each vertex. The _____ can also be called a regular hexahedron and is one of the five Platonic solids. It is a special kind of square prism, of rectangular parallelepiped and of trigonal trapezohedron.

Chapter 8. Radical Expressions and Equations

a. 2-bridge knot
b. -equivalence
c. -module
d. Cube

15. In mathematics, a _____ of a number, denoted $\sqrt[3]{x}$ or $x^{1/3}$, is a number a such that $a^3 = x$. All real numbers have exactly one real _____ and a pair of complex conjugate roots, and all nonzero complex numbers have three distinct complex _____s. For example, the real _____ of 8 is 2, because $2^3 = 8$.
   a. Cube root
   b. 2-bridge knot
   c. -equivalence
   d. -module

16. In mathematics, specifically group theory, the _____ of a subgroup H in a group G is the e;relative sizee; of H in G. For example, if H has _____ 2 in G, then intuitively e;halfe; of the elements of G lie in H. The _____ of H in G is usually denoted $|G : H|$ or [G : H].

If G and H are finite groups, then the _____ of H in G is simply the quotient of the orders of the two groups:

$$|G : H| = \frac{|G|}{|H|}.$$

By Lagrange's theorem, this number is always a positive integer.

If G and H are infinite, then the _____ of H is G is defined as the number of cosets of H in G.

   a. Inner automorphism
   b. Index
   c. Outer automorphism
   d. Even permutations

Chapter 9. Quadratic Equations

1. In mathematics, a _____ is a polynomial equation of the second degree. The general form is

$$ax^2 + bx + c = 0$$

The quadratic coefficient a is the coefficient of x^2, the linear coefficient b is the coefficient of x, and c is the constant coefficient, also called the free term or constant term.

_____s are called quadratic because the variable in the leading term is squared.

   a. Rationalisation
   b. Cubic function
   c. Difference of two squares
   d. Quadratic equation

2. _____ is the mathematical process of putting things together. The plus sign '+' means that numbers are added together. For example, in the picture on the right, there are 3 + 2 apples--meaning three apples and two other apples--which is the same as five apples, since 3 + 2 = 5.
   a. ADE classification
   b. AKS primality test
   c. Addition
   d. Abelian P-root group

3. In mathematics, a _____ of a number x is any number which, when repeatedly multiplied by itself, eventually yields x:

$$r \times r \times \cdots \times r = x.$$

In terms of exponentiation, r is a _____ of x if

$$r^n = x$$

for some positive integer n. For example, 2 is a _____ of 16 since $2^4 = 2 \times 2 \times 2 \times 2 = 16$.

The number n is called the degree of the _____.

   a. Cubic function
   b. Difference of two squares
   c. Rationalisation
   d. Root

Chapter 9. Quadratic Equations   41

4. In mathematics, a _____ of a number x is a number r such that r² = x, or, in other words, a number r whose square (the result of multiplying the number by itself) is x.

Every non-negative real number x has a unique non-negative _____, called the principal _____, which is denoted with a radical symbol as $\sqrt{x}$, or, using exponent notation, as x^(1/2). For example, the principal _____ of 9 is 3, denoted $\sqrt{9} = 3$, because 3² = 3 × 3 = 9.

   a. Square root
   b. 2-bridge knot
   c. -equivalence
   d. -module

5. In elementary algebra, _____ is a technique for converting a quadratic polynomial of the form

$$ax^2 + bx + c$$

to the form

$$a(\cdots\cdots)^2 + \text{constant}.$$

The expression inside the parenthesis is of the form x − constant. Thus one converts ax² + bx + c to

$$a(x - h)^2 + k$$

and one must find h and k.

_____ is used in

- solving quadratic equations,
- graphing quadratic functions,
- evaluating integrals in calculus,
- finding Laplace transforms.

In mathematics, _____ is considered a basic algebraic operation, and is often applied without remark in any computation involving quadratic polynomials.

There is a simple formula in elementary algebra for computing the square of a binomial:

$$(x + p)^2 = x^2 + 2px + p^2.$$

For example:

$$(x+3)^2 = x^2 + 6x + 9 \quad (p = 3)$$
$$(x-5)^2 = x^2 - 10x + 25 \quad (p = -5).$$

In any perfect square, the number p is always half the coefficient of x, and then the constant term is equal to p^2.

a. Reduct
b. Nested radical
c. Completing the square
d. Content

6. The _____ of a Lie algebra $\mathfrak{g}$ is a particular ideal of $\mathfrak{g}$.

Let $\mathfrak{g}$ be a Lie algebra. The _____ of $\mathfrak{g}$ is defined as the largest solvable ideal of $\mathfrak{g}$.

a. Cyclically reduced word
b. Class sum
c. Garside element
d. Radical

7. In mathematics, the _____s are an extension of the real numbers obtained by adjoining an imaginary unit, denoted i, which satisfies:

$$i^2 = -1.$$

Every _____ can be written in the form a + bi, where a and b are real numbers called the real part and the imaginary part of the _____, respectively.

_____s are a field, and thus have addition, subtraction, multiplication, and division operations. These operations extend the corresponding operations on real numbers, although with a number of additional elegant and useful properties, e.g., negative real numbers can be obtained by squaring complex (imaginary) numbers.

a. -equivalence
b. -module
c. 2-bridge knot
d. Complex number

8. In mathematics, an _____ is a complex number whose squared value is a real number less than or equal to zero. The imaginary unit, denoted by i or j, is an example of an _____. If y is a real number, then i·y is an _____, because:

$$(i \cdot y)^2 = i^2 \cdot y^2 = -y^2 \leq 0.$$

_____s were defined in 1572 by Rafael Bombelli.

a. Abelian P-root group
b. AKS primality test
c. ADE classification
d. Imaginary number

9. In mathematics, the _____ of a real number is its numerical value without regard to its sign. So, for example, 3 is the _____ of both 3 and −3.

The _____ of a number a is denoted by $|a|$.

a. Absolute value
b. ADE classification
c. AKS primality test
d. Abelian P-root group

10. In mathematics, the word _____ is a term for any well-formed combination of mathematical symbols. For example,

$$x^2 + 3x - 4$$

is an _____, while

$$)x) / 0$$

is not, because the parentheses are not balanced and division by zero is undefined.

Being an _____ is a syntactic concept - the meaning of the variables is irrelevant, but different fields have different notions of validity. See formal language for how _____s are constructed, and formal semantics for meaning.

Chapter 9. Quadratic Equations

a. Unit ring
b. Expression
c. Arity
d. Orthogonal

11. In mathematics, the _____ is a conic section, the intersection of a right circular conical surface and a plane parallel to a generating straight line of that surface. Given a point (the focus) and a line (the directrix) that lie in a plane, the locus of points in that plane that are equidistant to them is a _____.

A particular case arises when the plane is tangent to the conical surface of a circle.

a. -equivalence
b. Parabola
c. 2-bridge knot
d. -module

12. In mathematics, especially in the area of abstract algebra known as ring theory, a _____ is a ring with 0 ≠ 1 such that ab = 0 implies that either a = 0 or b = 0 (the zero-product property.) That is, it is a nontrivial ring without left or right zero divisors. A commutative _____ is called an integral _____.

a. Domain
b. Subring
c. Partially-ordered ring
d. Coherent ring

13. A _____, in mathematics, is a polynomial function of the form f(x) = ax² + bx + c = 0, where $a \neq 0$. The graph of a _____ is a parabola whose major axis is parallel to the y-axis.

The expression ax² + bx + c in the definition of a _____ is a polynomial of degree 2 or second order, or a 2nd degree polynomial, because the highest exponent of x is 2.

a. Vandermonde polynomial
b. Dickson polynomials
c. Factor theorem
d. Quadratic function

14. In linear algebra, the _____ of an n-by-n square matrix A is defined to be the sum of the elements on the main diagonal (the diagonal from the upper left to the lower right) of A, i.e.,

Chapter 9. Quadratic Equations

$$\mathrm{tr}(A) = a_{11} + a_{22} + \cdots + a_{nn} = \sum_{i=1}^{n} a_{ii}$$

where a_{ij} represents the entry on the ith row and jth column of A. Equivalently, the _____ of a matrix is the sum of its eigenvalues, making it an invariant with respect to a change of basis. This characterization can be used to define the _____ for a linear operator in general.

Note that the _____ is only defined for a square matrix (i.e. n×n.)

a. Trace
b. Dot product
c. Coefficient matrix
d. Defective matrix

15. A _____ is a three-dimensional solid object bounded by six square faces, facets or sides, with three meeting at each vertex. The _____ can also be called a regular hexahedron and is one of the five Platonic solids. It is a special kind of square prism, of rectangular parallelepiped and of trigonal trapezohedron.

a. -equivalence
b. -module
c. 2-bridge knot
d. Cube

16. In mathematics, and more specifically set theory, the _____ is the unique set having no (zero) members. Some axiomatic set theories assure that the _____ exists by including an axiom of _____; in other theories, its existence can be deduced. Many possible properties of sets are trivially true for the _____.

a. Abelian P-root group
b. AKS primality test
c. Empty set
d. ADE classification

17. In mathematics, the _____ of two sets A and B is the set that contains all elements of A that also belong to B (or equivalently, all elements of B that also belong to A), but no other elements.

For explanation of the symbols used in this article, refer to the table of mathematical symbols.

The _____ of A and B

The _____ of A and B is written 'A ∩ B'.

a. Intersection
b. ADE classification
c. Abelian P-root group
d. AKS primality test

18. In set theory, the term _____ refers to a set operation used in the convergence of set elements to form a resultant set containing the elements of both sets. As a simple example, a _____ of two disjoint sets, which do not have elements in common results in a set containing all elements from both sets. A Venn diagram representing the _____ of sets A and B. If one circle represents A, and the other B, then the red area represents the _____ of A and B. The area where the circles join, also shown in red, is the intersection of the two sets.

If we define two sets which contain unique elements; those of A not occurring in B and vice versa, then the _____ of these sets results in a set which contains all elements of A and B. In terms of notation, we could define this set operation as the following:

$$A = \{1,2,3,4\}$$
$$B = \{5,6,7,8\}$$
$$A \cup B = \{1, 2, 3, 4, 5, 6, 7, 8\}$$

Other more complex operations can be done including the _____, if the set is for example defined by a property rather than a finite or assumed infinite enumeration of elements.

a. Abelian P-root group
b. Union
c. ADE classification
d. AKS primality test

ANSWER KEY

Chapter 1
1. d	2. c	3. d	4. d	5. d	6. d	7. a	8. c	9. d	10. d
11. b	12. c	13. d	14. d	15. a	16. d	17. d	18. a	19. d	20. d
21. b	22. b	23. a	24. a						

Chapter 2
1. c	2. d	3. d	4. a	5. a	6. d	7. b	8. d	9. b	10. c

Chapter 3
1. b	2. b	3. d	4. b	5. c	6. c

Chapter 4
1. d	2. d	3. d	4. d	5. c	6. d	7. c	8. c	9. d	10. d
11. d	12. b	13. c	14. b	15. b	16. b	17. d	18. a	19. a	

Chapter 5
1. a	2. d	3. c	4. d	5. a	6. d	7. d	8. a	9. a	10. c

Chapter 6
1. d	2. d	3. d	4. d	5. c	6. d	7. c	8. d	9. d	10. d
11. d									

Chapter 7
1. b	2. d	3. d	4. a	5. d	6. c

Chapter 8
1. d	2. d	3. b	4. c	5. d	6. c	7. b	8. b	9. a	10. d
11. b	12. b	13. b	14. d	15. a	16. b				

Chapter 9
1. d	2. c	3. d	4. a	5. c	6. d	7. d	8. d	9. a	10. b
11. b	12. a	13. d	14. a	15. d	16. c	17. a	18. b		

www.ingramcontent.com/pod-product-compliance
Lightning Source LLC
Chambersburg PA
CBHW081220230426
43666CB00015B/2816